W9-CMI-046
3 0301 00036037 6

The Wisdom of the East

EDITED BY J. L. CRANMER-BYNG M.C.

THE POETRY OF LIVING JAPAN

The Poetry of Living Japan

AN ANTHOLOGY WITH AN INTRODUCTION BY

TAKAMICHI NINOMIYA

Professor of English Literature at Kobe University

AND

D. J. ENRIGHT

Lately Professor of English Literature at Kōnan University

John Murray

ALBEMARLE STREET LONDON

EDITORIAL NOTE

THE object of the Editor of this series is a very definite one. He desires above all things that these books shall be the ambassadors of good-will between East and West. He hopes that they will contribute to a fuller knowledge of the great cultural heritage of the East, for only through real understanding will the West be able to appreciate the underlying problems and aspirations of Asia to-day. He is confident that a deeper knowledge of the great ideals and lofty philosophy of Eastern thought will help to a revival of that true spirit of charity which neither despises nor fears the nations of another creed and colour.

J. L. CRANMER-BYNG

50 ALBEMARLE STREET
LONDON W.1

First published 1957
by John Murray (Publishers) Ltd
Printed in Great Britain by Butler & Tanner Ltd
Frome and London

CONTENTS

INTRODUCTION

At last the age of the new poetry arrived.

It was like a beautiful dawn. Some cried out as the prophets of old, others gave voice like the poets of the West. All seemed intoxicated with light, with new tongues, with new imaginings . . .

Our new poets were mostly simple-hearted sincere youths. Their art was immature, incomplete. On the other hand, they were neither vain nor pompous . . . Just think how novel speculations served many a young man instead of food and sleep. And think, too, how the sorrows and anguish of the modern world sent many a one out of his mind. I put aside my scruples, I joined in the chorus of these new throats . . .

Tōson Shimazaki
Introduction to *Poems* (one-volume edition, 1904)

With Tōson Shimazaki's first volume, *Seedlings* (1887), Japanese poetry was definitely launched upon a new career. Not that Shimazaki revolutionized either style—his language was exclusively pseudo-classical, in metre he followed the traditional alternation of five and seven syllables—or themes, for he still wrote of Nature, love and melancholy. What was markedly new was the feeling of excitement: here was a receptive soul, confronted suddenly with a fresh and vast view of poetry's potentialities. That, for instance, his 'Song of the Autumn Wind' was all too Shelleyan does not matter. What was important for the future was the very real imaginative liberation which Shimazaki experienced.

The Meiji era (1868–1912) was an age of marvels. Houses in Western style began to replace the thatched earthen-tiled ones; oil-lamps and gaslight appeared; restaurants ('resŭtoranto') proudly served Western food—milk, meat, bread and wine. The pass-word was 'Civilization and Enlightenment'. And the new age indeed required a new voice.

In 1882 the trail was blazed by a small collection calling itself *New Style Poems* and edited by three professors of Tokyo University (a philosopher, a botanist and a sociologist). The book contained translations of poems by Gray, Bloomfield, Campbell, Tennyson, Longfellow and others. Not, one would say, very strong meat for revolutionaries. But the title is accounted for (and justified) by the fact that in contemporary usage *Poetry* meant exclusively verse written in the Chinese style and *Song* applied only to the traditional Japanese *tanka* of thirty-one syllables. 'We regret that hitherto it was not our custom to write poetry in words of daily use,' wrote one of the editors. 'We have herewith introduced, after the manner of western poetry, verse of a new style'; while another remarked on the crippling shortness of the conventional forms: 'Facility in expression must mean shallowness of thought . . . How can a more consecutive thought be given vent in such short forms?' We quote this remark because Western readers tend to assume that the Japanese must find 'Western-style' free verse easier than their own tight traditional forms. Such is not the case. The fifteen syllable *haiku* is probably the easiest verse-form in existence; while, on the other hand, Japanese poets soon found to their cost that, as T. S. Eliot said, 'no *vers* is *libre* for the man who wants to do a good job'.

The propositions advanced in *New Style Poems* were soon seized upon. One monument to them is a narrative poem in 679 lines on a Biblical legend. However, the other Western influences —relating not to size but to form, language and subject-matter —have been much more significant. And the reaction against facility and shallowness was strengthened by further books of translations, such as Ōgai Mori's *Semblances* (1889), which included Goethe, Heine, Hoffmann, Byron and Shakespeare.

This was how matters stood when Shimazaki made his *début*. His appeal was immediate and widespread, though he encountered opposition from the nationalist camp who found his work lacking in the masculinity which they attributed to the more dignified Chinese-style poetry. From that point of view, Bansui Tsuchii was a more pleasing writer: though his themes were often exotic, he invariably preserved the 5/7 syllabic rhythm (even translating Homer thus) and favoured Chinese phraseology. In retrospect his seems the first (and perhaps the last) voice of the samurai class in modern poetry. The 'feminine', which Shimazaki and his followers were supposed to stand for, was of more enduring value, for it was more flexible, more ready to go forward into a changing world.

A third book of translations must not be omitted here, for it was certainly the most important to date. A young man, Bin Ueda, was solely responsible for *The Sound of the Tide* (1905), containing 'fifty-seven poems by twenty-nine poets—three Italians, four Englishmen, seven Germans, one Provençal and as many as fourteen Frenchmen, of whom the late Parnassians and the present Symbolists form the greater part'. The author also said in his preface, 'It is as if, where the ancient well-trodden path comes to an end, an open uncharted field of briars lies before us. But those who would disparage a courageous pioneer are either cowards or sluggards . . . Beware! The constellations in the heaven of Poetry have shifted position!' The volume offered little in the way of metrical innovation, but the translator's handling of the language—his modification of literary-Japanese—deeply affected the major contemporary practitioners.[1] 'The translations of Bin Ueda offered good nourishment, a mixture of high-minded Parnassians with the nearer Symbolists, old Hugo along with new Samain,' a later critic comments. 'Bin's was an

[1] See *Japanese Literature*, by Donald Keene (John Murray), p. 18.

influence greater than any mere study of poetic history because the impact was immediately upon the sensibility.' We may smile at the collocation of Hugo and Samain, but such odd accidents are common in intercultural relations.

Of the four most prominent poets of this time, Kyūkin Susukida is often called (somewhat uninformatively, we may think) the Romantic-Parnassian in contrast to Ariake Kambara, the Romantic-Symbolist. (The Japanese, it should be mentioned, are very fond of such resonant categories.) And in fact there is not much of the *parnassien* about Susukida, whereas his romanticism is seen in his yearning for things remote in time. In the European sense, it is equally doubtful whether Kambara could be described as a symbolist. Both poets were accused of 'obscurity', both attempted to please with a plainer sort of verse, and both ceased to write at an early age. In their stead appeared another pair of 'symbolists', Hakushū Kitahara and Rofū Miki. The essence of Kitahara's poetry was described by a contemporary as 'kineorama' (a compound of 'kinema' and 'panorama'). His first volume, *Heresy*, had as epigraph a parody of Dante:

> Through me to the languors of *melodia*,
> Through me to the garden of sensuous pleasures,
> Through me to the bitter stupor of the nerves.

His concern was with the intensely sensuous (his favourite colours are red, black and gold); what he listened for in 'Heresy' was its secret, precious music; what he sought out was the mysteries that came from 'the wonderlands' of the West. With this volume and his later *Recollections* (less colourful but perhaps healthier) he made himself the most widely read of all the modern poets. By contrast, Rofū Miki looks rather thin. He expelled *melodia* in favour of straightforward visualism; what he would restore, in place of the 'wonderlands' and Baudelaire's diabolism, was the 'elegant' and the 'wholesome':

> Among the rampant weeds
> The elegant is smothered;
> In this pale blue light
> The wholesome cannot stay.

The following era, Taishō (1912–1926), saw the first world war and Japan's rise to the status of a world power. Modern poetry had by now established itself, so that Shimazaki would no longer have felt that 'the name of a "New-Style Poet" was like a crown of thorns upon our heads. It meant damnable ridicule, unbearable contempt . . .' Looking back, we are struck by the fact that, although the Taishō poets may be less than great, they are conspicuously individual in character.

It was Mokutarō Kinoshita who led off the period: musician, painter, *Kabuki* playwright, doctor and connoisseur of wine, he was a born dilettante. He formed the 'Pan Society', which met in a tavern kept by a fellow aesthete. Sipping at a tumbler or liqueur glass—exotic beverages!—he gazed through the window at the turbid canal, a relic of Yedo culture. Never losing himself in drink or in poetry, he was a very conscious artist. Kōtarō Takamura, on the other hand, was sober by nature, almost a puritan, and he was one of the few Japanese poets who could really *think* in poetry. Probably his most considerable contribution was his establishment of colloquial free verse, a style already experimented with, as a working poetic mode. It is often said that his success in this mode was helped by his unfamiliarity with the Japanese tradition and his four years' sojourn abroad, but the fact remains that it came naturally to his straightforward unsophisticated temperament. (Verhaeren, whom he translated, was his favourite poet.) His poem included here, 'My Poetry', is a good corrective to the view that Japanese 'Western-style' poets must necessarily forfeit their national distinctiveness.

Bochō Yamamura turned from theology to become a violent experimentalist, but his *divertissements* and his 'gibberish' are more substantial than the organized antics of the surrealists whom he anticipated. Sakutarō Hagiwara's sensitiveness sometimes amounts to morbidity—we are aware of exposed nerves—but there could be no doubt about the lively originality of his first volume, *Baying at the Moon* (1917), and his fresh handling of the colloquial style. 'All new poetic styles since have issued from this book', he later claimed with some justification. Actually his own 'colloquialism' represented a reaction against the prolixity and sloppiness which marred much current usage of the style, for it is taut and condensed and in some points partakes of a return to the old literary style. Saisei Murō is very different: 'a sentimentalist, as pure-hearted as a young chestnut leaf with silvery down', as his friend Kitahara put it. His style is a curiously clumsy one—as it were, a literary style rebuilt on the basis of the new colloquial one—but it fitted the tearful sorrows of an adolescent mind which were its theme, and the resulting 'new melodies' had a tremendous success. Yet another personality of the age was Haruo Satō (who later married the first wife of the novelist Junichirō Tanizaki: the affair is referred to in two poems printed here). He is generally held to offer a return to the lyricism of Shimazaki, for he resorted almost exclusively to the literary style in his more important poems, yet this old-fashioned element is always accompanied by a rather incongruous modernism in the play of intellect.

In addition to the above poets, sometimes lumped together as the 'Art School', we must mention briefly the 'People's Poets', men of good will and humanitarian ideals, who were however guilty of superficiality in both their thinking and their deployment of colloquial free verse. But one important outsider is Kenji Miyazawa, a devout Buddhist and a chemistry teacher in a northern district. Religion, Nature and Science were the triple basis of his poetry, and his 'Mental Sketches' (as he would have his poems called) are as crisp as the icy northern air.

To close this survey of the Taishō period we should mention the 'Japan Futurist Movement' with its special syntactical and typographical arrangements or derangements. Expressionism, Cubism, Fauvism, etc., followed and each had (often in combination) its followers. Perhaps the only writer to survive this vortex was the dadaist, Shinkichi Takahashi, whose work has a desperate sincerity about it.

The Shōwa era, the Age of Universal Peace, coincided with universal war. Between the wars democratic ideas had made some progress before being crushed out of shape between the upper millstone of militarism and the nether of class-warfare. Not surprisingly, the majority of literary intellectuals favoured the workers' cause; and the poetry of the period is most conveniently considered under the two headings, the Social School and the Art School.

The Social poets stem from 1903 when Kagai Kodama published his (immediately banned) *Socialist Poems*, 'marching songs against the world of great evil and the disease of gold'. Takuboku Ishikawa, famous as an innovator in the old *tanka* form, started as a Romantic and ended as a socialist, writing what he called 'Edible Poems'. And the socialist poets achieved both a wide public and a majority in the Poetry Conference (1917–1926), an attempted amalgamation of Japanese poets out of whose protracted collapse grew a diversity of schools and movements which this introduction cannot enumerate. We should however cite the dadaist-anarchist *Red and Black* group, with its slogan

'Poetry is a bomb', and the Marxist magazine *Battle Flag* (1928). The only figure who really established himself in this noisy and confused period was Shigeharu Nakano, whose syncopation of lyrical and prose rhythms well suited his rigorous and dryly satirical mind.

The first poets to enter the stage after Japan's defeat were those who had refused to collaborate with the regime and had been imprisoned or rendered silent. Nakano's poems were republished, unexpurgated. Tōsaburō Ono, previously an anarchist, worked on his poetics—'the negation of the lyrical'—as exemplified in his volume *Osaka*. Of post-war socialist poets in general, it can be said that, in spite of their undiminished preference for society rather than the individual, they are less fanatical in declaiming against their opponents and more liberal in their views on poetry. Their chief hope now seems to lie in the 'Circle' poets, recruited from among factory hands and school-teachers: more than two hundred 'Circle' poetry magazines are now being published.

So much for the Social School. In dealing with what we have called (rather crudely) the Art School, mention must be made of an influential collection of translations, *A Group in the Moonlight*, by Daigaku Horiguchi (1925). Nearly seventy poets were represented, all French and all recent, most notably Apollinaire, Jacob, Jammes and Cocteau; and the poet Tatsuji Miyoshi has since remarked, 'It was a wonder, a delight. It was as if one had suddenly been shown into a gallery crowded with pictures of *les esprits nouveaux*.' Another equally decisive event was the magazine *Poetry and Poetics* which appeared in fourteen quarterly volumes of over two hundred pages each between 1928 and 1931. Here was introduced the latest work of Western writers; as the editor, Yukio Haruyama, later reflected, 'Valéry and Cocteau and Jacob and Morand, Soupault and Aragon and Breton and Eluard and Radiguet, Eliot and Joyce and Pound and Huxley and Lawrence—all flowed at once into our world; it was a wonder, a thrill, almost breath-taking! We were saturated with the whole atmosphere of the age.' No wonder that a good deal of indigestion resulted—yet how else could Japanese poets nourish their art?

From these two influences emerged three schools: the Lyrical, the Realist and the Intellectual. Junzaburō Nishiwaki is considered the leader of the Intellectuals, and his attraction lies in the combination of difficult thought ('ambiguity') with crystal-clear imagery ('Morning up-turned like jewels'). The Intellectual group were particularly interested in poetic theory; and the magazine *New Domain* (shades of *New Country*) translated essays and poems by Spender, Day Lewis, Michael Roberts, Herbert Read, Auden, MacNeice and others.

The Realists were presided over by Shimpei Kusano—a Japanese *fauve*, as he is called, though his favourite beast is the frog ('the hundredth class' is how he describes this animal, in reference to the 'fourth class' or proletariat). The chief common principle of the Realists was their rejection of the Intellectuals' excessive theorizing. And by far the most significant of the three groups under discussion was the Lyrical, whose organ, *Four Seasons*, printed eighty-one issues between 1934 and 1944. Among the members were several of the poets included in this anthology: Kaoru Maruyama, Tatsuji Miyoshi, Katsumi Tanaka, Michizō Tachihara, Shizuo Itō and Fuyuji Tanaka. They campaigned equally against the preoccupation with theoretics of the Intellectuals and the crudeness and superficiality of the proletarian writers; and, while profiting from modern developments, they sought to stabilize poetry by a judicious reference back to native traditions—as it were, a reconciliation of the wisdom of the West with that of the East.

The post-war years are too near to be seen in any proper

perspective, though one is still aware of the large overall division between those who place the stress on 'Art' and those who place it on 'Life'. But poets are now having to take a wider, less exclusive view of these two conceptions. After three-quarters of a century of dispute and struggle, they have learnt that poets are not only born but are also made; that neither the old artlessness nor the new artfulness will do any longer.

Little magazines (sometimes not so little) have always been a prominent feature of the modern poetic scene, for Japanese writers are much keener than their Western colleagues on groupings, alignments and manifestos. Since the war the leading magazines have been revived, among them Kusano's *History in the Making* (the old Realist organ), the veterans' platform *Gala*, which has printed Nishiwaki, Shirō Murano and Ichirō Andō, and the imperishable *VOU*. The latter, to be read as 'Vow', was founded by Katsue Kitasono in 1935 and maintained ties with Ezra Pound and others. Conspicuous among the new groups is *The Waste Land*: this magazine, started in 1939, was resuscitated in 1947 and now appears as a yearly anthology under the title *Waste Land Selections*—it cannot be said that Japanese poets seek to conceal their indebtedness. Its present influence is considerable: whether salutary or otherwise remains for the future to decide.

The production and dissemination of poetry is such today that no less than three hundred magazines (in addition to the two hundred 'Circle' magazines) are in circulation. Add to this the fact that the traditional forms, *tanka* and *haiku*, not only have survived but are more popular than ever, and one must agree with the old saying, that Japan is 'the land blessed with the Genius of Speech', doubtful though that blessing sometimes is. The one current magazine which stands for catholicity is *Poetic Studies* (*Shigaku*). Besides publishing established writers, *Poetic Studies* brings out special issues of *Review of Local Poetry Magazines*,

Beginners in Poetry and a Year Book. It is a matter for congratulation that at least one major magazine, standing outside the groups and movements, should be watching for new and perhaps solitary talents.

Our aim in the anthology which follows has been to illustrate the course of modern poetry in Japan by translating work that is, firstly, good in its own right and, secondly, amenable to translation. Merely experimental or merely imitative work, whatever its historical interest, we have thought best not to inflict upon the reader at this time. Both the selection of poems and the introduction have been affected by considerations of space, and we are aware that there are omissions from both. In assuring that representation was as proper as possible, and in the composition of the introduction, we are greatly indebted to a group of scholars and poets connected with the magazine *Kropes*, published in Kobe: among them in particular, Masami Ogawa, Yasuo Ochi and Toshikazu Yasumizu. Also, for advice on particular points of interpretation, to the staff of the Japanese Literature Department of Kobe University. We are grateful to the poets and copyright-holders for permission to print these translations and to Professor Mikio Hiramatsu for help in obtaining this permission.

THE EDITORS

It should be mentioned here that the heavier part of our joint labours fell on Mr Ninomiya, who was responsible for literal drafts and elucidation. No theory of translation underlies our work. We were merely concerned to find a working compromise between what the poet was saying in Japanese and what could decently be said in English. Over a period of time we moved through decreasingly literal drafts to what, but for the congratulatory sound of the word, might be termed 're-creations'.

By way of compensating for the loss of the musical qualities so potent in Japanese verse, we have not hesitated to bring out more clearly a meaning or to sharpen an occasional image. In every case, however, the final version was checked against the first literal draft as a form of control. Lastly, in rendering Japanese names we have followed the Western practice of placing the given name before the surname.

D. J. ENRIGHT

The letter [n] in the text
refers to Notes on pp. 95–97.

Tōson Shimazaki

Otsuta

I crept into being as faintly
As blossoms glowing in a night of spring.
Dim in my memory, a pair of shadows,
My father and mother faded away.
And so I was left, an orphan, a shadow
Of shadows, alone and helpless—
But for a youthful priest, who took
Me in. And now I am a maiden,
With my hair put up, and my heart
Stuffed full of vague longings.

The young priest said:
If you desire to taste it at its best
Do not pick the persimmon fruit too early . . .
I was so glad to hear him talking thus,
And hastened to reply:—now is mid-autumn,
See how the autumn looks! . . .
I offered a persimmon to the sage,
And with his lips against the fruit he said:—
I never knew how deeply coloured a persimmon is;
Why did you not tell me before?

The young priest said:
If you desire a long and healthy life
Do not indulge in drinking *sake* . . .
I was so glad to hear him talking thus,
And hastened to reply:—drinking is relaxation,

Look here and see the colour of spring! . . .
I offered the sage a cup of *sake*,
And with the cup against his lips he said:—
I never knew how delicious *sake* can be;
Why did you not tell me before?

The young priest said:
If you desire to tread the narrow path
Do not lend ear to the sirens' song . . .
I was so glad to hear him talking thus,
And hastened to reply:—songs reflect the singer's
heart,
Listen now to what it says! . . .
I offered the sage a tuneful song,
And with his soul in ecstasy he said:—
I never knew how charming a song can be;
Why did you not tell me before?

The young priest said:
I am one who is searching for Truth,
You must not tempt me out of the Way . . .
I was so glad to hear him talking thus,
And hastened to reply:—love is one of the ways,
Look where it carries you to! . . .
I pointed to my breast,
And trapped by passion the sage then said:—
I never knew how sweet it is to be in love;
Why did you not tell me before?

One autumn evening
As we were walking out together,
We came across a stone and picked it up . . .

We found it white as snow.
The young sage said:
Why, this must be the Philosophers' Stone;
I love its colour very dearly:
I will treasure it up, out of men's sight, for
ever . . .

In the Birdless Country

LIKE two bats in the birdless country,[n]
Sōsuke, with a spade across his shoulder,
Kōsuke, with a net in his hand—
Sōsuke off to the mountain, Kōsuke to the sea.

Cucumber-flowers in bloom, cool dews
On mulberry leaves along the mountain path,
Cicadas' songs in the evening shadows—
Kōsuke, on the sea, dreams enviously of these.

Boats drying out on the beach, seaweed
Scattered along the sands, the voice
Of summer's sea heard among wave-tossed weeds—
Sōsuke, on the hill-top, dreams enviously of these.

This is the world of change—a change indeed!
Kōsuke, now, with a spade across his shoulder,
Sōsuke, in turn, with a net in his hand—
Kōsuke off to the mountain, Sōsuke to the sea.

Mist opens the day, and frost will close it;
Swift as thought, the spring is past, and autumn too.

Our dreams are like wild flowerlets,
The blown sand buries them from sight.

As swift and brief
Are youth's vague hopes—where are they now?
Look back, and nothing now is left
Of Sōsuke's or of Kōsuke's dreams.

The lilies are back once more,
And green plums hanging on the trees.
In the glaucous shadows, with irresolute footsteps,
Sōsuke returns, along with Kōsuke.

Crafty Fox

THERE in the garden, a little fox
Steals out at night, when no one is about,
And under the shadow of the autumn vines
He eats in secret the dewy bunch.

Love is no fox,
Nor you a bunch of grapes.
But unbeknown my heart stole out
And plucked you in secret, when no one was about.

First Love

WHEN I saw you, your hair newly put up,
Under the bough of an apple tree,
I formed a picture of you as a girl in flowers,
Wearing a flower-comb above your forehead.

When you reached out a soft white hand,
And gave me an apple—a fruit of autumn
Tinged with rose—then I knew
I was deep in love, my first love.

When the sigh I failed to hide
Lightly stirred your hair,
From the cup of love you gently offered
I sipped my fill.

Under the bough of the apple tree
A lane had grown before we knew.
You ask, who was the first to tread it?—
A simple question that shakes my heart.

A Coco-nut

FROM some far-off unknown island
A single coco-nut is washed ashore.

How long have you roamed the waves
Since leaving your native land?

Is the parent palm still green,
Its leaves still offer welcome shade?

I am a wanderer too, no shelter but the beach,
Alone, not knowing where to lay my head.

When I press the nut against my breast
I feel once more that desolate longing.

Watching the sun as it sets in the sea
Strange tears in a strange land soak my cheeks.

My thoughts are borne across the eight-fold waves
Back to my native land—oh when shall I return?

Bansui Tsuchii

The Moon on the Ruined Castle

When in spring they viewed the blossoms from the turret,
  Wine-cups passed round, reflecting the moonbeams
    That gleamed through the boughs of the ancient pines—
      Where are they now, those beams?

When in autumn the frost lay white on the camp
  And one by one the crying geese were counted in flight,
    Bright upon rows of drawn swords the light was seen—
      Where are they now, those beams?

And now upon the ruined castle the moon of midnight—
  For whose sake shines the moon as bright as ever?
    Only the ivy still entwines the walls,
      Above the pines the raging wind alone is singing . . .

That heavenly radiance has remained unchanged;
  Only on earth are vicissitudes suffered—
    Is it to lighten them, that now
      Ah, the midnight moon shines bright on the ruined
        castle?

Fair Japan

Now spring is far behind with its pink mist of overflowing
  blossoms,
And brocaded autumn, strewn with red leaves and chrysanthe-
  mums, is also on the wane;

But the Fifty-three Stages along the Tōkaidō
Are the living images of the prints of Hiroshige—
The snowy mornings in the ancient capital,
The mountain range that lies behind, with its Thirty-six Peaks,
And below them the River Kamo,
So bare and gloomy at low-water, in the winter-time,
Yet often enlivened by the vernal gaiety of music and singing . . .

For a hundred leagues the San-yō sea-shore runs to the west,
Where lonely havens and long beaches, one after another,
Each with a new curve, succeed, the sea and the hills
Revealing their exquisite forms.
No lovelier, in truth, is the sight of Messina or Naples:
There, at the foot of Mount Etna, they boast of Taormina
(True vestige, they tell you, of Greater Greece);
And here we have the Bay of Miho—
Under the shadow of the great hibiscus, Mount Fuji,
Capped with perpetual glittering snow—
The Bay of Miho, famed for the Hagoromo robe
That a fairy danced in, a fairy from the moon,
Long ago on the beach, long ago;
Over the western strip of sea is the Yaba Gorge,
Renowned for its rocks, carved by a deity's chisel;
Equally famed, the ravine of the Tenryū River
Breaks inland for miles, from the Tōkai shore;
Away to the north-east, among undulating mountains,
Is Lake Towada, inset like a lucid mirror, a fairy pool:
The traveller will recall Lake Maggiore.

At the land's edge in the north-eastern region,
A mountain, taking its name from 'Gold', defies
With its giant rocks the wrath of the ocean;

Alongside race dark-green tides, for thousands of miles
Across to the continent of America.
Springing from the depths of the southern seas
The Warm Current, vast in extent, bears its numberless
  sea-sprites
To the shore—it clashes with the Cold Current from the
  Sea of Okhotsk:
The ocean churns and rages,
Clouds well out, waves heave, and gales break loose—
This is where the Tuscarora Trough lies, unplumbed.
For all its name of 'Pacific', the maddened water here
Prevails, the billows beating at the sky—
Well may they totter, the great ships, the castles of the sea!
But enough of struggle, confusion and turmoil—
The small bay of Matsushima, 'Pine Island',
With its islet clothed in a hundred pine-trees,
Beams like a smile.

Ah, high are the mountains and limpid the streams,
Deep and unruffled the pools which they form!
Who is there but knows it?—
The fame of exquisite Matsushima,
Image of the fabled elysium of Horai—
Far away in the east,
A thing of such beauty—could it long be hidden?
The cynosure of wonder, to which are turning
The longings of millions, east and west alike.

Kyūkin Susukida

Were I in the Province of Yamato[n]

Were I in the province of Yamato, now in October . . .
I would follow a lane through the wood of Kaminabi, with its sparse-leaved trees,
To Ikaruga, at dawn, the dew on my hair—when the tall grass
Ripples across the wide field of Heguri like a golden sea,
And the colour fades from the dusty paper-window, and the sun is faint—
Between the wooden columns, insatiably, I peer at the golden letters of the precious age-old scriptures,
At the ancient Korean lyre, the grey unglazed pottery and the gold and silver paintings on the wall.
This is the Shrine of Everflowering Arts, the inner sanctuary fragrant with burning incense,
Whose fumes intoxicate me, like an urn of nectar.

On the terraced fields along the newly opened road,
Reddish mandarine oranges glimmer between the leaves—it is midday,
When you might turn at the pleasing sound of a tranquil song
And discover a yellow warbler, hopping on a bough like a pigmy musician—
Light of feather, hovering airily, a roaming leaf,
In the hedges and among the trees—
Can it be a spirit of the fields, disguised?
From deep in the twilit temple comes the sound of a sutra—
Hearing it, some careless stroller of old
Might have thrilled through his being . . .

The sun is low now, behind the trees, and people
Cluster quietly together in the garden of the Dream Palace,
Where dry crinkly leaves scuttle along, the leaves
Of maples, nettle-trees and broad-leaved bo-trees . . .
Silently the corridor is listening
To the murmur from the street; turning back,
You will see high pagodas, their tarnished spires dyed by the sun's
 last rays,
Which the flowers too throw back—an evening scene
Recalling the old days, when Buddhist monks
Softly trailed their long robes on the ground behind them . . .
Ah, were I in the province of Yamato,
This day in October, and this hour of evening,
Then for a moment at least, I should have shared
In the souls of the saints, myself!

In the Heat of the Day

THE time is midsummer,
The hour is noon—
The sun shines white
On the ears of corn,
The sun spatters
Across the track,
The sun seethes
Like raw foaming *sake*.

In a small meadow
A line of trees
Dangle their leaves
Like limp arms;

The stagnant bog
With its green scum
Is dazzled now
And breathes its last.

A flake of cloud
Gasps and wavers
And shudders past
And disappears;
The azure sky
Seems nothing but
A vacant grave!

The surface scum
Is now warmed over;
The newt bores through
The bottom filth;
Stunned by the smell
Of the dusty earth
The snake retires
Beneath the grass.

That solemn Wrath
That rules on high—
Lonely indeed!
Nothing more proud
Than that inexorable Soul,
The Sun
Of the month of June!

Home Thoughts[n]

My home is where the warm sun shines on the Cicada River,
Where the countless birds sing on the boughs the livelong day—
On the day of the equinox, the Festival of the Dead, town-girls stroll to the temple
And girls from Katsura, fishing the restless trout downstream,
Smell pure wine in the drops that fall from the fishing-net—a broad spring day,
When young men row back from the cherry-viewing in the slow sound of oars,
Talking with their loves in the shade of the young trees,
While the boy-players of the Mibu farce,[n] with expert comic gestures, spread laughter among them—
Let us return there, you and I.

My home is where young camphor leaves diffuse their dim perfume,
In early summer the broad-leaved oaks wave their limp arms in the breeze,
Along the lane through the gold-green shades of the wood of Tadasu
A lacquer-shafted ox-wagon quietly moves—and there sits
The Imperial Messenger, on his way to the Hollyhock Festival,
In a court hat, adorned with a talisman twig.
Or in June, at the Gion Festival, when the sun shines white
On the roofs of the floats that creak along the city streets, flooded with spectators—
Priests from Hiei Temple, flower-girls borne along among them . . .
Let us return there, you and I.

My home is where blown maple leaves scuttle about in November winds,
On frosty mornings in the fields of Makuza, and some of the pious monks,
Coming to town on a halcyon Day of Congregation, are lost and homesick towards evening,
On their way back, while showers fall, wet-eyed and lonely,
In the southern outskirts—short is the day, and sad,
But the youthful votaries, absorbed in the treasure-house,
Bend over the sacred sutras, in the shade of the Buddha's dusty image,
And dream in the russet evening light of the Golden Shore beyond . . .
Let us return there, you and I.

My home is where black alders flutter their yellow leaves, in wind, along the path through the paddy,
Where the brown cows tread homewards to the soft singing of the country girls,
As the sun's last rays doze off in the evening, leaning afar towards some pagoda's spire—
There stands a tree whose leaves begin to fall—doleful as a hired mourner idly adjusting her veil,
And the moon can just be seen, casting a dreamy glance aside;
As the blue clangour of the bells begins, the pilgrims yearn for those they have left at home . . .
Let us return there, you and I.

Ariake Kambara

When the Wise Physiognomist Looked at Me

When the wise physiognomist looked at me today,
'Dim and inauspicious are your brows,' he said.
'Beware—before the sky of this enthralling passion
Is overcast and torn apart by gales—and stay away!'

'Stay away,' he told me—ah! from your tender presence,
From the rising wave of your soft black hair—
Softer than the undulating green of the meadows . . .
What do you say to this verdict of his?

Close your eyes, you will see at the end of the endless beach
A shadow that moves in the twilight, with hanging head—
You will see a ravenous beast on the prowl!

And that is it—the shadow fleeing from you,
Painted in the colour of melancholy, treading a path of thirst . . .
But no—rather the fragrant whirlpool and the dazzling storm!

The Oyster Shell

An oyster in his shell
Lives in a boundless sea,
Alone, precarious, limited,
How miserable his thoughts . . .

Unseeing and unhelped,
He sleeps behind a sheltering rock.

But in his wakeful moments he must sense
The ebb and flow of the infinite deep.

Though the turning tide at dawn
May flood in to its height,
The oyster's being, destined to decay,
Is tied to a narrow shell.

The evening star, so luminous,
Turns the waves to crests of corn:
Us it reminds of a distant dove—
Of what avail to him?

How sad a fate! Profound, unbearable,
The music of the ocean
Still confounds him day and night.
He closes tight his narrow home.

But on that day of storm
When woods along the sea are shattered,
How shall it survive—the oyster shell,
His shelter, left to die a destined death?

Hakushū Kitahara

The Precious Music of Heresy

I meditate upon the heresy of the degenerate age—Christianity's magical Deus;
On the Kapitein of the Black Ship, the wonderlands of the Red-haired,
The crimson glass, the sharp-scented carnations,
The figured silk of the Southern Barbarians, and the arak, vinho tinto and the other wines . . .

Even in my dreams I see blue-eyed Dominicans, reciting their canticles,
Talking of the strange banned God, of the bloodstained Crux,
The deceitful device that shows the poppy-seeds as big as apples,
Or the flexible optical instrument through which the paradisal sky is viewed . . .

Houses are built of stones, and the white blood of their granite,
Contained in a diamant glass jar,[n] is said to glow at night . . .
And the visions of Electriciteit, in a fragrant smell of velvet,
Shadow forth, I learn, the quaint birds and beasts of the lunar world.

I am told that the cosmetics there are distilled from the flowers of poisonous herbs,
And oh the image of Mary, even, is painted with putrid petrolic oil![n]
Moreover, the pale-coloured letters of Latin and Portuguese that run sideways,
How full they are of sensual sounds, sweet and sad . . .

Grant us, then, enticing Reverend Fathers—
Though a hundred years were contracted into one moment, and
one should bleed to death on a cross,
What care I?—Grant us this day your secret of secrets, the exotic
carmine dream.
O Deus! this I beg in yearning prayers that burn me, flesh and
soul . . .

Okaru and Kampei [n]

Okaru weeps . . .
Like a velvety hollyhock quivering in the lingering twilight,
Like the soft touch of felt,
Like the daylight fading from a field of buttercups,
Like a puff-ball softly afloat in the air . . .

She weeps and weeps and still the tears flow:
Kampei is dead, Kampei is dead,
Kampei the darling, so young and so handsome—
Kampei has committed *harakiri*!

Okaru weeps as she thinks of the smell of the youthful flesh . . .
A keen stimulant, she reflects, as strong as the onion in the malt-
house;
The lambent feel of his skin recalled the open light in May,
His breath was as heated as hot black tea.

Held close, she saw the midday salt-field flash with blue,
Her nerves, as white as parsley, were taut, then faint, then
withered;
The tremulous inside of his thigh, the lips that he sucked . . .

On the day of parting, his white hand smelling lightly of gunpowder,
Just before he entered the palanquin, as she sliced fresh vegetables
ready for pickling, deeply absorbed . . .

This Kampei is dead and gone!

Like an orphan in a greenhouse,
Okaru, excited by a medley of sensual memories,
Luxuriates in her distresses.

(Through the windows of the puppet theatre can be seen the red berries of spear-flowers glittering in the setting autumnal sun, and from below the hazy yellow city streets comes the whistling of river boats.)

Okaru weeps . . .
Accompanied by the heart-breaking samisen,[n]
Beautifully manipulated and in utter abandonment,
Rising upon the swell of the chanter's voice,
She weeps and weeps, as if to drown herself,
Okaru weeps . . .

(Colours, and odours, and music . . .
Who cares what happened to Kampei . . . ?)

Spinning-Wheel

SPINNING-WHEEL, spinning-wheel—quiet and deep hums the
hand-spinning;
How wistful the evening, when the spinning-wheel is softly
turning!

Two *abóboras,*[n] golden and red, lie on the wooden floor,
On the wooden floor of the Community Medical Centre—
How lonely she is, the old caretaker, sitting there all alone!

—Deaf and blind. But now that May is here,
How sweet the faint and dusty smell of the scattered cotton!
The white skeleton in the glass case—how strangely solitary;
The moonlight along the canal—how modestly it slants aside!

Spinning-wheel, spinning-wheel, calm and silent is the hand that
spins,
How wistful the evening, as her thoughts are softly turning!

Rofū Miki

Native Place

My native place—
A field of trees
Under the moon
Faint sounding flute

The girl
Her heart on fire
Listened once
And tears fell

Ten years passed—
In that same heart
Do you still weep
A mother now?

After the Kiss

'Are you asleep?'
'No,' she says.

In May,
And midday
Blossoming.

Under the sun
On the grass by the lake,
'I'd die like this, eyes closed,'
She says.

Bell Across the Snow

At dusk, upon my heart
The snows of memory fall—
Soft and tremulous,
Monotonous and drear.

Buried griefs sleep underneath:
My voice closed up and covered in,
I place my breast against the burning tomb . . .

Yet how melodious the bell now sounds,
How tears refresh, when once they're shed!
The soft chime trembles out . . .

I dream
Of how I'll tread my boundless way . . .
The wind that blows along the dale
Subtly stirs my heart awake . . .

Even this sunset, sorrow-silvered,
Bends a faithful smile on me.
Oh green grass!—
Tender shoots among the snow there,
I would come yearning forth like you,
There, over there, with delicate hands . . .

Song of Departing May

I see—
In the recess of the ruined garden
The blossoms scatter intermittently, in silence—

The footsteps of the wind,
And in the gentle light of afternoon
The back of sweet departing May . . .

Soft blue is the sky all over,
And in the dreaming trees
The birds are singing vainly . . .

Now, in the garden,
Memory hangs her head
And sheds her secret tears—
While Time,
Along a path of wistful scents,
Cradling his tender thoughts,
Already leaves his happy home behind . . .

Departing May—
I see your back . . .
Glitter of tiny insects, creeping things of earth,
The drone of swarming honey-bees . . .
Amid the glitter and the hum turned golden
And dreaming in the grief-choked sun,
Amid it all, May is departing,
Beautiful May!

In the recess of my ruined garden,
Near the pond where mosses flourish
And saffron blossoms flutter down,
Lonely blossoms, forming folds of silence,
Drifting, floating in the sun—

There a single dragonfly, blue-gleaming,
Fixes his pupils in a settled stare.

Departing May—
I see your back . . .
Farewell to the blue stare of the dragonfly,
Farewell to the fluttering saffron blossoms—
Time takes his leave of the midday pond . . .

Mokutarō Kinoshita

Sherry

Tranquillity, the winter night,
And on the stove the water simmering . . .
A faint flush rises to my face—
Is it illusion, the ear's imagination,
That as I gaze into the heeltap of the sherry
I seem to hear a distant human voice,
And voices sobbing in the distance?

'Why? Oh why . . . why i-i-s it
That you-ou-ou . . . ?'
Can it be Roshō[n] that is singing?—
This spring I heard her in Kyoto, in a music-hall,
Rending her listeners' hearts—
Or is it the alcohol?

In the calm of the winter night
The sherry is auburn-clear.
Can it be Roshō that is singing,
Or is it the alcohol?
Pushing the curtain aside, I watch
The star-lit night across the Koamichō banks,
A solitary barge . . . the light sound of the water.

(*To the Host of the bar*, Maison Kōnosu)

Ryōgoku

PASSING under the Ryōgoku Bridge
A big ship lowers its main-mast;
'Here we go!' the boatman cries . . .
The fifth of May, and a dampish chilly wind.
The fast boat from Yotsume[n] glides along with slow strokes of the oars;
Settling on the printed peony of the Garden livery,
A butterfly sways to the waves . . .

Kikumasamune, the fabulous Nada *sake*—
Into the thin-walled tumbler I pour the old familiar fragrance . . .
Upstairs in a European restaurant
I gaze at the twilit sky at sunset,
Over the dreamy dome of the Kokugikan Wrestling Hall,
At the far-off bird in flight, the shadow of the evening bird.
My heart is ill at ease . . . but why?

This Side and That Side

ON that side of the street a woman passes,
Her hood drooping over her eyes;
On this side a man is walking—
He looks cold.
This is the evening stroll, in a lonely street,
And they seem in no hurry at all—
Even though they are strangers,
Why don't they walk along together . . . ?

Kōtarō Takamura

My Poetry

My poetry is not part of western poetry;
The two touch, circumference against circumference,
But never quite coincide . . .
I have a passion for the world of western poetry,
But I do not deny that my poetry is formed differently.
The air of Athens and the subterranean fountain of Christianity
Have fostered the pattern of thought and diction of western poetry;
It strikes through to my heart with its infinite beauty and strength—
But its physiology, of wheat-meal and cheese and *entrecôtes*,
Runs counter to the necessities of my language.
My poetry derives from my bowels—
Born at the farthest limits of the far east,
Bred on rice and malt and soya-beans and the flesh of fish,
My soul—though permeated by the lingering fragrance of Gandhara[n]
And later enlightened by the 'Yellow Earth' civilization[n] of a vast continent
And immersed in the murmuring stream of the Japanese classics—
Now marvels excitedly at the power of the split atom . . .
My poetry is no other than what I am,
And what I am is no other than a sculptor of the far east.
For me the universe is the prototype of composition,
And poetry is the composed counter-points.
Western poetry is my dear neighbour,
But the traffic of my poetry moves on a different path . . .

Taciturn Sea Captain

I'M making another trip,
Way past the Southern Cross.

Well, yes,
When the wind blows in earnest, it blows in earnest . . .

No, I'm not scared—
The roundish world out there is too unhuman for that . . .

That's what I like—
There's a fish that screams, 'What use—humanity?'

All humbug!
I've never feasted on Wonders or Mysteries!

Reality, just that—
That's what weighs and weighs upon us . . .

How do I look?
Sad, and gay, and something more besides . . .

Really winter now!
Smoke from the roofs along the water-front, not many
people about, mountains white . . .

Well, be seeing you, then.
Hey, the cigarettes—don't leave them behind!

The Rain-beaten Cathedral

Another squall!
Looking up at you, the collar of the overcoat
Lifted against the slanting rain—It is I,
He who makes it a rule to come at least once each day—
The Japanese.

This morning
A terrible storm, increasing since daybreak,
Now rages in the four corners of Paris.
I cannot distinguish east from west,
Nor even which way the storm is moving, as it runs amok, here
in the Ile de France . . .
But here I am again,
Oh Notre-Dame of Paris!
Soaked with rain,
Just to gaze at you, to touch you,
To steal a kiss from you, your flesh of stone.

Another squall!
It is the hour for morning coffee,
But when I looked down from the Pont Neuf on my way,
The barges were still on the leash, like puppies, along the banks
of the Seine;
The autumn-bright leaves of the plane-trees
Like so many finches driven by a hawk
Were scattered in a flutter of light . . .
And when their branchy heads are jerked and tossed
The horse-chestnuts there behind you
Send their grey starling leaves scurrying in the air—
The pelting rain and the contrary wind
Dash them, like arrows, down on the stone-paved square.

The square is patterned all over now—
Running silver broken by islets of gold-umber leaves.
The roar of the torrent vibrates in the pores of the skin,
Howling, grating . . .
Though human voices are dumb
The other creatures of Paris join in this outcry!
In the shower of golden plane-tree leaves
I stand, in the middle of it all.
No different the storm in my native country,
Except for your towering presence!

Oh Notre-Dame, Notre-Dame!
Cathedral like a rock, a mountain, an eagle, a squatting lion—
A hidden rock in a mist,
The bulwark of Paris,
Pelted by blinding rain,
Buffeted head-on by the beating wind,
You rise up before me, oh my Notre-Dame of Paris!
It is I, who look up at you,
The Japanese.
My heart thrills at the sight of you;
Before the semblance of heroic tragedy,
This youthful heart, come from a strange and different land, is
over-full—
It throbs irrationally, trembles in time with the screaming air.

Another squall!
How they rage, the four elements, striving to efface you, to turn
you back to nothingness!
Rain splashes in smoke and phosphorescence;
The scaly spotted cloud grazes against your peaks;

The entwining cyclone seeks to snatch in its claw just one of
your belfry pillars;
Beyond count, tiny bright fluttering elves collide, burst and
stream on the tracery of the rose-windows . . .
The gargoyles, glimpsed through the splashes high on the edge
of the building—
They alone bear the brunt of the fluttering mob of elves,
Lifting their paws and craning their necks,
With bared teeth, voiding the fiery stream of wind and rain . . .
Rows of curious stone saints nod to each other, with odd
gestures,
Huge buttresses on the sides lay bare their arms as ever,
And the storm beats on those slanting arcs with all its force!
The peal of the organ on the day of Mass!
What has become of the cock on the thin high steeple?
Fluttering curtains of water are falling on all sides now—
And you stand in the middle of it all . . .

Another squall!
And there at the heart of it
The Cathedral, firm with the weight of eight centuries—
Millions of stones, laid one by one by the hands of age-old faith,
Gigantic scaffold of truth and belief, reaching to eternity . . .
You stand alone and dumb,
Stand and resist the might of the storm;
At the mercy of the elements,
Knowing the power of nature, yet you preserve your calm, as
long as the earth remains unshaken.
Oh the flesh of stone, rusted, grey, iron-blue, gleaming with rain!
With my hand upon it,
I feel as if I touched the white hand of Esmeralda—
Esmeralda, in the monster's company,

Storm-loving hunchbacked Quasimodo, who may be lurking in some corner at this moment—
That ugly body bore a righteous soul,
Possessed the strength of steel;
Ruffians, bullies, mockers, evildoers,
Above all, petty people and their gossiping—all their blows he caught on his silent back,
He deemed himself but dust in the service of his God . . .
It was you who bore this monster!
And how many more have since been born?—
No longer hunchbacked or grotesque, but normal healthy Quasimodos,
Bred in this tender bosom of yours, solemn and full of a mother's protective love . . .

The rain-beaten Cathedral!
After a pause, another squall, in *allegro*—
Down swings the baton in a sudden flash,
And all the instruments of heaven are in commotion—
All round, the chaotic revolutions of a rhapsody . . .
And in the midst of it, oh Cathedral, towering in sheer silence,
Watching intently over the roofs of storm-ridden Paris!
Do not take it amiss
That someone stands here now,
A hand against your corner-stone,
A fevered cheek against your flesh—
It is I, drunk with beauty,
The Japanese!

Bochō Yamamura

Solo

View of the sky
At twilight,
And my past life—
The sadness of it;

Across the sky
Birds of passage
In their enormous world
Have gone—no one knows where . . .

The Curve

At the bottom of the river
In the afternoon
A moving motor-car—
Giving a fish a ride
And running it over—
Causes a brilliant disturbance.

In the Blue Sky

In the blue sky
Fish were swimming.

In time with my sighs
Deep drawn
Fish were swimming.

Fins of the fish
Were glittering.

Here, there,
Aimlessly,
Lots of fish were swimming.

In the blue sky
Fish were swimming.

And those fish
Had each a heart . . .

An Old Pond

THERE is an old pond in the hills:
The pond is a man in prayer—
Still is the water,
And in the mirrored sky
The cloud—how lonely!
Startled by the rustling wind
A water-bird has plunged
Down to the very bottom—
The one cloud in the sky is quivering . . .

With its brilliant setting sun,
Its bird,
Thus bobbing up and down—
This is the pond of the human heart,
Where loneliness lingers on.

There is an old pond in the hills:
The vision of the water
And the solitary bird . . .

Sakutarō Hagiwara

Late Autumn

THE train was passing overhead,
And my thoughts meandered into the shade.
Looking back, I was surprised to find
How my heart was at rest!
Streets were strewn with the autumn sun's last
 rays,
Traffic crowded the highway.
Does my life exist at all?
Yet in the window of a humble house,
Along a back street where the smoke still hung,
Purple hollyhocks were blooming.

Night Train

MORNING's dim twilight
Looks chill through the finger-traces on the window,
And the mountain ridge dawning pale white
Is as silent as quicksilver.
The travellers lie half-awake, dreaming . . .
How dreary! The tired electric lamps sigh inconsolably.
The sweet tang of the varnished woodwork
Or the cigarette smoke that curls faintly
On a tongue made tasteless by the night's journey—
Wretched enough,
How much more lonely a wife in a strange place!
Haven't we passed Yamashina yet? . . .

And she, turning the valve of the pneumatic pillow,
Furtively lets the air out . . . a feminine act!
Suddenly nestling together in grief
We look out of the window at the breaking dawn
And find, in an alien countryside,
Blooming columbines, white, white!

A Leisurely Indulgence

Walking in a grove of pines
I saw a café, cheerful-looking—
Far away from the city streets,
No one came to visit it.
Secluded among trees, it was a café
Reminiscent of dreams . . .
Blushing as if for love, the girl
Brought me a special dish,
Refreshing as an early morn . . .
I took my time, then lifted up my *hōku*,[n]
And ate omelette, fried fish and suchlike.
White clouds were floating in the sky—
It really was a leisurely indulgence.

Woman!

With lips painted lightly pink
And powder smelling white and cool about the
neck hair—
Woman!
With your breasts like rubber balls,
Don't press too hard against my chest,

Nor with your whitebait fingers
Tickle my back so cunningly—
Woman!
Ah, with a sigh so scented,
Don't gaze too closely into my eyes—
Woman!
Drop your little tricks—
Woman!
You are sad,
Because you can never do without them.

Tortoise

A GROVE,
A swamp,
And an azure sky:
Weighing ponderously upon one's hand
A pure-gold tortoise quietly sleeps . . .
This bright unhappy Heaven-and-Earth
He bears in pain,
And probingly sinks through one's soul . . .
The tortoise sinks in the deep azure sky.

A Sick Face below the Surface of the Earth

BELOW the surface of the earth a face appearing,
A sad invalid face appearing.

In the dark below the surface of the earth
A grass stem softly starting to sprout,
A rat's nest starting to sprout,

Countless tresses entangled,
The nest beginning to tremble;
And at the winter solstice
On the sad sick surface of the earth
Beginning to grow, the roots of green bamboos
Beginning to grow,
Looking terribly pathetic,
Gossamer-web,
Terribly, terribly pathetic . . .

In the dark below the surface of the earth
A sad invalid face appearing . . .

Saisei Murō

Lonely Spring

THE sunbeams drip, drip, incessantly;
Half asleep, the water-mill turns and turns;
In the sapphire sky
Far off are seen the Echigo mountains—
So lonely . . .

No word heard or spoken all day long,
I walk the fields.
Away into the distance
Undulate the rape-seed flowers—
Now it is more than ever
So lonely . . .

Susaki Waterfront [n]

Do not come out in the broad daylight!—
The light will make your pale forehead ache.

In sleep your face resembles sulphur;
That old familiar forehead—it resembles death.

On the wintry Susaki waterfront I woke, alone and
 sad;
Groping about me, I found chill flesh . . .

Driven from my lodgings, I had no home to go to;
With bowed head in the last tram,
I heard with you the midnight winter sea . . .

The tram came out of the breaking day;
And I had no home to go to . . .
Far off, in the pale sky, geese were flying.

Towards the Susaki waterfront my thoughts are
turning:
Ah, what is she doing now, in the metropolis?

Haruo Satō

Song of the Samma [n]

Alas,
Autumn wind!
Have pity—tell
How a man, alone,
At supper this evening,
Is eating *samma*,
Lost in thought . . .

Samma, samma—
Eaten with a sprinkling of juice from a sour mandarine—
That is the custom in his native place.
Oddly amused by it, how often the woman
Has picked a green mandarine for the supper table!
Ah, when a woman soon to be left by her husband
Sat at table with a man whose wife betrayed him,
The little girl whose father was a brute,
Fumbling with her little chopsticks,
Held out her *samma* guts to him who was not her
father . . .

Alas,
Autumn wind!
You surely saw
That unusual picture of domestic happiness.
Come now,
Autumn wind,
At least bear witness
That those moments of happiness were not a dream!

Alas,
Autumn wind!
Have pity—tell
The wife restored now to her husband,
Tell the child no longer fatherless
—That a man,
Alone this evening at his supper table,
Is eating *samma*,
Is in tears . . .

Samma, samma—
Bitter, is it not, and salty
Taking *samma*, hot tears sprinkled on it!
Eating *samma* thus—which country's custom is it?
Alas,
How nice to know . . .

To a Person

LAST night was the second time you have appeared in my dream:
Your husband, however, has done so no less than six times . . .

With you I find little to talk about, even in a dream:
With him, however, I walk and talk and am merry.

Even the dream world, I find, is against me;
Hence my doubts as to the Other World . . .

After both dreams I wake and cannot sleep for long;
Your dream, though, is ephemeral—

Whereas your husband's always lasts too long,
And leaves me with a headache on the morrow.

I confess how much I wish to see
Your husband killed by me in my dream—

And wish to see
How much I shall regret the killing . . .

A Wish

POINTLESS, without meaning,
Short-lived—
But true.
An extraordinarily true poem—
If one of these days
I could write just one of that sort!
Now I know what God intended,
When he made a cloud.

The lullaby
That once my mother sang—
If I could bring it back entire!
But she has long forgotten it—
Sung on the moment's spur.

Once in my life-time,
If only I could write
An air-like song, free and unobtrusive,
Yet striking directly at the bowels of men,
All superfluities at once disgorged,
And lasting as long as humanity lasts—
Just one of that sort, if only I could!

Kenji Miyazawa

Sapporo City

Upon the far-drifting flood of grey
And on the sand of the square of the twisted town
I sprinkled my sorrows,
Like so many green fables
Which the little birds had no desire to peck . . .

Orchard

White-bearded Dr Yamada goes home with books under his arm;
Twilight creeps silently along; the shoots on the trees softly unfold.

Birds soar, the air weighs heavier; my toothache is more than I can bear;
Windows spring out blue-lighted; blue are the sighs that recite the clumsy *De-kli-na-tion* [n] . . .

Fantasia Under the Clear Sky

At the Mizusawa Observatory

At the farthest point of the cold bright azure sky,
On the right shoulder of the heights of Taneyamagahara,
A conic form is seen,
In shape akin to the head of Buddha.

Exhausted by mathematical calculations,
My eyes at first are surprised at the apparition
Of a secret tower in a strange aerial expanse,
But find, after all, it is merely water and air,
A dazzling cumulus, and nothing more . . .

To some, though, this is not the whole story.
Right along the bluish edge of heaven,
The peaks and ridges of palaeozoic soil
Armoured in blazing ice and snow
And the basins and the valleys—
All contain some legendary tree or barrow,
Each by tradition the dwelling place of a demon.
And if you wilfully fell the tree
Or open up the barrow into arable land
Or pick too many irises thereabouts . . .

Yes, on such a lovely windless day as this,
Well might one be carried off,
Into the seemingly quiet pile of eight-fold agate clouds,
And there hung upside-down in the brilliant air,
Stabbed through and through by spears in unseen hands
Or beaten and crushed in the head or breast
And left for dead . . .
Many still believe this, and fear it still.

But now to me, unseen,
It seems as if the fourteen stars of the day
Are cutting through the cobweb strands of the celestial
globe,
And the Andromeda couple are quietly passing by—

So mellow the light
Of the emerald sky
That my eyes are renewed,
And I dare to enter the dismal door
To stoop once again
Over the scribbled mass of mathematical calculations . . .

Silent Wail

WITH all of us nursing you—
Must you still prolong the agony of life?
While I, having lost my hold on the tremendous Faith,
Having divested myself of purity and suchlike humble
    items,
Now walk in the sombre bluish world of the Asura.[n]

Are you treading the destined path alone?—
While I, your sole companion in the selfsame Faith,
Am weary and wretched, out of the bright ascetic Way,
Adrift in fields of hemlock and fluorescent fungi—
How far can you manage, by yourself?

    'I don't look pretty, do I?'
With what pain and resignation in your smile
You bravely question Mother;
Your eyes too sharp to miss
The slightest change in my expression.
    'No, you look quite pretty, child,
    Today you look your best!'
Yes, indeed,
Your hair glows darkly,
Your cheeks are like a child's, like apples—

Go with those pretty cheeks
To be reborn in Heaven!
    'But my body smells bad, doesn't it?'
    'No, never!'

No, it could not!
Rather, these are summer fields
Full of the sweet smell of small white flowers . . .
Only, I cannot say that now
    (I who am walking in the Asura world).
If my looks are sad
It is that I am gazing at this double heart of mine . . .
Ah, do not turn away
Your bitter eyes from mine like that!

Shinkichi Takahashi

The Raven

Staring into the deep darkness
I see a raven.
It has a beak, and sinewy feet.
And the greedy way it pecks at the field is
    abominable.

With fierce swells of solitude at its back
The tide presses forward, howling like a tiger,
It snaps at the distant rocks.

In all likelihood its feathers are black as coal,
Its heart as hard as iron.

I wish I could drown this insolent bird in the sea;
I cannot rest till I have burned it up like coal . . .

The Fine Rain

In the morning as the fine rain falls
A phantom dog comes creeping along.

Making tea and drinking it alone,
I have a phantom cat jump on my lap.

For a moment, in a dream lane,
I plant bamboos, lay flat stepping-stones, and
listen to the wind.

The cloud scurries by, and it is night;
I close the tangible window and go to bed.

Shigeharu Nakano

Locomotive

He has a giant's frame,
He weighs ten thousand pounds of blackness,
His body is measured out . . . his every inch,
His pipes and wheels and countless nuts and bolts are rubbed and polished inside and out.
When he moves
The hands of meters are quick to turn;
When he runs
The rails and the sleepers shake;
And when his piston-arms begin to stretch,
When they shuffle to and fro and spin the wheels,
And when I see him sweep through towns and villages,
My heart starts throbbing,
Tears fill my eyes . . .
With a brass plate at his front
And a red lamp hanging out,
He is always emerging out of smoke, carrying a thousand lives.

Flags and signals
Wave him on . . . on shining rails in perfect order . . .
To the back of this big and honest man
We raise our arms in eager praise.

Tokyo Imperial University Students

SALLOW faces,
Some in spectacles,
Some in *haoris*,[n]
Some in *rubashkas*,[n]
Some in overcoats . . . with buttons three inches
in diameter,
Some as shabby as beggars . . .
And they walk down the Ginza,[n]
When drunk, they lapse into deliberate use of
indecent vernacularisms.
'Profundity of learning,
Cultivation of character . . .' And
'*What Suffering Symbolizes* is not so bad!'
Pfui!
They parade in and out of the great Main Gate;
Some specialize in football . . .

Tōsaburō Ono

Winter

In the stove the fire has fallen.
We have already talked about
Whatever is to be talked about—
Talked, and left nothing to be said,
Left not a question to be settled.

And yet—
How dissatisfied these hearts of ours remain!
Friend—with your head drooping in the up-turned
coat-collar—
Do you know
How languid the truth is that is only proved by
words?

Nature-Hater

The names of the trees,
The names of the grasses,
Are not too familiar to me;
Nor the names of birds and insects—
I have forgotten them all.

With the aid of scant knowledge and a feeble memory,
I look at the plants in the field, I point at the crops,
I call to the birds . . .
Nature makes no response.

I have long done without it all.
Then this morning I saw over the reclaimed land,
Suddenly soaring into the sky, something like a lark
(Isn't it called a lark?).
There is neither tree, grass, bird, insect, nor anything any
more.

I have filled up the void of memory
With 'Mori', 'Noguchi', 'Ayukawa', and other such
names . . .[n]

Fuyue Anzai

Birthday Again

I pinned a butterfly against the wall—no more flitting about. Happiness I pinned as well . . .

On the table a ribboned fowl, in the shape of the fowl.

In the bottle the water, in the shape of the bottle.

In her chemise she, in the shape of her beauty.

The Warship 'Mari'

1

The warship, which bore the name *Mari*, lay at anchor again, at moon-rise, at a wharf in North China—secret and as white as rock-salt.

I was the Captain, a lieutenant, slim and fair, with the figure of a gazelle;[n] I seemed to myself as graceful as a woman. I lay upon the morocco divan in the Captain's cabin, drowsing by day and by night, obsessed by opium and utterly abandoned. All this while a snow-white collie at my feet kept watch over me. I had been unable—I do not know how long—to move at will. I was a prisoner.

2

The moon-rise reminded me dimly of my sister—my only sister. I had an inkling of her fate. Long now she had been violated by the vicious Chief Engineer of this ship, from Normandy. But I was powerless. Moreover, the *Mari* was now a ship that shifted anchorage from port to port under cover of darkness —a ship of the fleet, under the command of infamous Yellow Pirates . . . Against my will I was slipping into an innocent sleep —a sleep that was not exactly sleep.

3

Midnight. I awoke to the ominous creaking of the pulley. Once again someone was being consigned to the sea—I had a vision of the wooden coffin sinking down towards the dismal water. Sharper than the flash of steel, I suddenly visualized the body of my sister, now a corpse. I struggled to get to my feet, but the snow-white collie, as cold as a button, was holding me down on the divan . . . Alas! Impotently I writhed my feeble body, and then fainted.

4

The moon had slithered down like an almond. Black night reigned—time for the *Mari* to weigh anchor. The ship swung round on its ram, under cover of darkness, the colour of the plague.

The Gulf of Tartary and a Butterfly

SITTING cross-legged in a wooden chair, I nose at the muzzle of a gun. Smelt in the pale cerebrum, the gunpowder bears me off into the three-dimensional inner world . . .

The rickshaw which carries me is climbing a slope along a park. Under the cloudy sky the merry-go-round is on the point of starting, and the horses are lining up their leather ears. But the rickshaw is already emerging out of the cloudy sky, gaining the summit of the ascent . . .

I must acquiesce in this autonomous marching on . . .

Her eyes are closed; she presses the side of her face against the map that hangs on the wall. Sliding along her shoulder, the haggard Gulf of Tartary flows like a shawl.

That slanting look of hers always implies indignation. I take no notice.

I continue with the lesson, notwithstanding.

To give the lesson, I walk up and down.

To walk up and down, I pause. Thus engaged, her face at last breaks into a smile for me.

The smile abruptly invites a projectile—the projectile stitches her to the Gulf.

Another second and her whole system will be dissolved. Through the hole made, the Gulf will pour down in torrents. And how shall I hold myself together?

I make up my mind.

The releasing of the safety-catch sounds like the clipping of tickets at a provincial station.

I level my gun, take careful aim at her . . .

When a butterfly flies up and quietly covers the muzzle.

Fuyuhiko Kitagawa

The Rush Hour

At the wicket
The finger is clipped together with the ticket.

Festivals

Curiously enough
I like
The aftermath of a festival.

In the midst of the festival
In the throng of people,
I seldom lose myself.
I look on—
I only look on.

But when the festival is over
And the people have all dispersed,
I find myself hanging about
Where their merry-making was most
extravagant,
And am always surprised
At myself . . .

Again,
Curiously enough,
I like
To help prepare for a festival.

Faces in the Procession

THE procession, its back turned to us,
Was proceeding in good order.
The clear stream
Mirrored the shadows on its white sand bed.
The line of trees gazed inquiringly down upon it . . .
The procession proceeded in good order.
After it
The dogs
Followed in a mass, without barking . . .
But all of a sudden,
As if it had smelt its owner,
A dog sprang up
And snapped at the hem of somebody's coat.
Though the hem was about to be ripped off,
The wearer would not turn round.
The dog began to bark—
At each bark
The hem
Fell free from the dog's mouth.
Then the dog pounced on it again.
At this moment
The procession, its back turned to us,
All at once turned its face about—
Startlingly expressionless masks of faces!
Just the selfsame face, each after each . . .
Then all of the dogs—
Not only the one that tore the hem—
But all of the gathered dogs
Shivered in unison,
Dropped their tails on the spot
And cringed.

Iku Takenaka

Japan for Sightseeing

Fujiyama—on sale!
Miyajima—on sale!
Nikkō—on sale!
Naruto, Aso—
All on sale!
Nippon—everywhere on sale!
Please, please! Come and see!
I rub my hands . . .
I smirk . . .
Money—much, much: the more the better.
Nipponese—all buy motor-cars.
Nipponese—all fond of lighters.
Nipponese—all clever gardeners.
Nipponese—all singers of popular songs.
All make kowtows.
All, all, very meek—yes, yes!

(*1949*)

At the Close of Day

It is far into the night.
The clamour of my beloved town has ceased, and my finger has ceased to turn the pages. The tiny, tiny feathers of Time alight on my eyelids.

Turning the switch near at hand, I lean upon the darkness, as if upon the bosom of my mother. Noiselessly I mingle with the thick darkness. Just for the moment I yield up to someone else the form given to me . . .

The moment, like that of the close of a life, makes me instantaneously grow immense, immense. It is then that I start slowly encircling the whole globe . . .

Memory of a Witch

In snake-coloured tights
Tightly fitting her to a T,
She made her entrance on the stage.

Her pupils were mobile,
Her arms were bare,
Fragrant the back that was turned to me.

I was five or six at the time.
Shouting some musical charm,
'Hey presto!' she shot her pistol.

Innumerable cards flew out of her mouth;
A blindfolded girl floated through the air;
A negro in a coffin was cut in half . . .

That night I could not sleep:
I wished to follow her wherever she might go.
How can I forget those eyes, that voice!

In the paper, 14th November 1944,
I find her obituary notice in a corner,
In No. 7 type, looking somewhat diminished—

Her real name, Katsu Nakai, born in Tokyo,
She was a disciple of Tenichi, and died at the age of
59 . . .
Ah, the witch who first planted the seed of love in me—
Tenkatsu Shōkyokusai, turned to dust, turned to a
luminous worm . . .

Jun Yamamura

Gay Summertime

Enticed by a beauty on a railway poster,
Papa, who suffers from piles, vouchsafes to visit the sea.

The sky is heartily blue, and the wartime boom
Has swollen the summer colony; the sea is hot to boiling.

In the backyard of a seaside inn the washing flutters,
From early morning a plump-armed maid grinds at the pump . . .

The town is busy switching on and off its lights, for air-raid practice,
While the boys in khaki complacently knock back beer.

But somehow the autumn can be smelt around us.
Oh, bony Mama with her gay cosmetics!
Striped shafts of dazzling sunlight are touched with purple,
All day with butterfly-nets children are chasing clouds.

The Story of a Dream

The first streaks of dawn are faint
On the morning of the first day of the year.
My wife, her brow cut deep with years of care,
Adds to her age another new year.
Her face is resplendent with joy;
Taking her fan out, she offers to dance.

She asks consent of those in the other room—
They are silent.
She asks again in a louder voice,
And is answered with jeers.
Tears stand in her eyes . . .
Moved to pity,
I was about to favour her with a little money,
When the dream dissolved away.

TATSUJI MIYOSHI

Snow

SENDING Tarō to sleep—it slowly blankets Tarō's roof:
Sending Jirō to sleep—it slowly blankets Jirō's roof.

Nostalgia

LIKE a butterfly, my nostalgia . . . The butterfly flies over hedges, sees the sea around the afternoon street-corner . . . I hear the sea inside the wall . . . I shut my book; I lean against the wall. It strikes two in the next room. 'Sea! Far-off sea! . . .' I write down on the paper: SEA. In our language you contain a 'mother' in you.[n] And MOTHER—in the language of the French, you have the 'sea' in you!

Sea-gulls

AFTER all, freedom is theirs . . .
The sky is where they make love,
The clouds are where they lie . . .
Freedom is theirs, after all.

After all, freedom is theirs . . .
Their eastern wall is hung with the sun,
The morning sea is their dining room . . .
Freedom is theirs, after all.

After all, freedom is theirs . . .
Their western window is hung with the sun,
The evening sea is their dancing room . . .
Freedom is theirs, after all.

After all, freedom is theirs . . .
They are their own native land,
They are their burial place . . .
Freedom is theirs, after all.

After all, freedom is theirs . . .
One star is their dwelling place,
One tongue is enough for their speech . . .
Freedom is theirs, after all.

After all, freedom is theirs . . .
The morning glow is their song at dawn,
The evening glow is their song at dusk . . .
Freedom is theirs, after all.

The Deer

In the morning wood a deer reclines,
The shadow of its antlers on its back.
A gadfly follows its trajectory
Straight to the ear arrested by a distant stream.

Junzaburō Nishiwaki

Rain

A lissom goddess came with the south wind:
She wetted the bronze, wetted the fountain,
Wetted the belly of a swallow, its golden hair;
She embraced the tide, licked the sands, and drank
the fishes;
She wetted in secret the temples, public baths and
theatres . . .
And those dishevelled platinum lyre-strings—
The tongue of the goddess—
Softly wetted my tongue . . .

Let the Traveller Pause

Let the traveller pause!
Before you wet your lips
At the meagre trickle here,
Think, Life's traveller—
You, too, are a mere water-sprite
That dribbles from between the rocks.
This thinking water does not flow for ever,
At some point in eternity it peters out . . .
A jay is singing noisily.
Sometimes, out of this very water,
A phantom rises, crowned with blossoms:

Life Eternal is a dream, useless to pursue it;
Into the murmuring stream of life ephemeral throw all
your cares,
Till at last you vanish off eternity's cliff:
This is the reality, this the real wish—

Thus speaks the phantom *kappa*,[n]
Who leaves his watery home and comes to villages and
towns for sport,
When water-grasses grow in the shade of floating clouds.

Shimpei Kusano

Queroqué the Frog: An Autobiography

I was born in the suburbs of Bologna,
In a lotus pond.
Standing on his head and kicking the sky—
The sight of a grebe
Was a source of amazement to me.
My name is Queroqué—
A title conferred by myself, of course.
One day I was caught in a net
And borne straight off to a university;
To the Galvani Laboratory, in fact.
Some students (as it transpired)
Passed by, humming a barcarolle—
On that afternoon, in the year 1780,
A scalpel was applied to my abdomen,
And the world conceived the idea of the electric
current.
I was dead,
I was out of this world,
The Italian heaven was very, very beautiful.

Conversation on an Autumn Night

Chilly.
Isn't it chilly!
The insects chirrup.
Yes, they do.
Soon have to go underground.

Oh, I hate to go underground.
You get thin.
So you do, considerably.
What is it exactly that bothers me?
Stomach, I imagine.
Shall we die when we have done with
    our stomach?
Oh, I hate dying.
Chilly!
Yes.
The insects chirrup.

The Frog

Your dream
Is beyond the horizon of peaks;
Your back
Is a trap for the heavens . . .

(Yes, that's right.)

Shūzō Hishiyama

High Summer

Under the weight and depth of the brightness of the clear sapphire sky, and over the desiccated stubborn stubble—the sunflower now stands, tall and swaying, in dribbles of golden oil and sweat all over stem and leaves, as it turns and turns with the sun. Suddenly there are cicadas chirping incessantly—a wind upon the flower's oil and fire . . . And in me, too, the days and years that I have let slip by, attended now by abundant shades and light, come surging back, surging back . . .

Sumako Fukao

Will-o'-the-Wisp

With an alarming big voice,
Won't someone knock at my door?
With sturdy shoulders beneath a black mantle,
Squaring those manly shoulders below—
Won't someone call on me?

Like an old dotard,
The day monopolizes the autumn,
Under the sun there is nothing but sighs;
And loneliness unbearable
Has struck the grasshoppers dumb.

Stranger! Stranger!
Take me, won't you take me
Where Time, like a bouquet, brings delight,
To that city, full of wonders,
Where I burn to go?

With a deaf old woman
Who doesn't deign to answer
I have lived too long:
It is time, yes, time
To say goodbye.

Won't someone help it!—
The child is crying
For the doll that danced so well dances no more.

Find a new spring for the one that is broken,
Find a new toy, a surprise, for the girl.

Still they are waited for—
The footsteps I know it is idle to wait for—
Poor ears!
Don't you know that Loneliness,
Burning blue in a will-o'-the-wisp,
Has just crept through the rickety door
And out of the house?

Dante's Scourge

At his Tomb

BEFORE Dante's Tomb, where the sun dedicates his everburning rays, I prayed to be truly human—that, if this were granted, I would not ask to be a poet.

Dante handed me a silver scourge—the famous scourge, supreme definition of high indignation, the scourge with which he whipped his fatherland so bitterly that his arm ached. I shook it, promising in my heart never to use it on a mere pack-mule.— I suddenly stood upright.

Holly leaves abounded in Dante's Garden, and to their thorns I was now most sensitive. Like a woman new-born I signed in the visitors' book—Your humble maid-servant, Sumako Fukao . . .

Kaoru Maruyama

Distant View of School

Ten-odd years I have journeyed since leaving school.
Turning about, I see at a great distance in my memory
The school like the relief on a small shiny medallion:
The blocks of classrooms are crowned with tiers of earthen tiles—
And a teacher is speaking.
Young faces, fixed in one unanimous stare, are listening to him;
But next to a window someone is looking aside,
Just as I did, looking abstractedly this way—
Hasn't he noticed me yet?
Alas, I can see him so clearly from here . . .

A Gyroscopic Lamp

Once I took a fancy to the ship's lamp, lighted on a night voyage. It swayed to the incessant motion of the waves, yet always returned to its point of balance . . . As a boy I always dreamt of being a sailor.

How many years ago!

The hurricanes of this human world have blown and blown on the sails of my life, and yet the gyroscopic lamp between my ribs has still kept upright the faint flame of my poetry.

Fuyuji Tanaka

Mosquito Net

It is autumn now.
Before one is quite aware, it is autumn,
And time to get out the white-papered *shōji*[n] in the morning and the evening too.
We shall soon have done with the mosquito nets,
In a few days they will be put away . . .
The dark green colour, the red cloth hems
And the metal rings to hang it by, that clink and rattle when you fold the nets . . .

When you lay your tired body on the white bedding,
How delightful the fine green shadows streaked along it
As if on the slopes of a hill!
And when you awake at midnight,
A clean-shaven moon
Is softly treading over the dark green waves . . .

One night a star, like a woman's heart,
Was sticking to the net:
It tickled my heart.
Wasn't it one of those nights
That were sultry and feverish?

When at nights
The rain patters past, as if the drops were grass-seeds,
I enjoy the cool feel of the mosquito net
Against my naked feet;

Immersed in its peculiar fragrance
I hurry on my path of thoughts, alone . . .

But when, like filtered bean-curds,
Dawn spreads across the dwindling night,
The dream-filled net will sway
Like a ghost above its native hemp-field,
And take me, half-asleep, will take me back to sleep . . .

It is autumn now.
Before one is quite aware, it is autumn,
And time to have done with the mosquito nets.

Stone Staircase Overlooking the Sea

My hands lie on her shoulders.
'We can see the sea from here!' she says, turning.
My hands drop, like a crab's claws . . .
The vivid sea of early summer is seen through the summer-orange bush;
I turn my eyes towards it,
But at once they are fixed on the nearer objects—her hair, her profile . . .
To make up for the hands, deprived of her touch now, as heavy as if they were artificial.

Shizuo Itō

Evening Sea

Slow but steady, the twilight and the incessant
Dull crests close in upon me from the rough grey surface.
At the top of the lighthouse, hardly noticed, a green light
 starts.

It takes a long, long time for the aimless light
(So reminiscent of some useless presentiment)
To be made brighter and brighter by the darkness.

But by and by, because of the all too regular revolution
And the tireless blink of the green light, how wearied
The sea will have to lie the whole night through!

Picture Drawn by a Boy

Red-edged
Big blue crucifers
One by one fill the universe—

Pretty flowers! So many of them!
No, Mammy, they're STARS!

A line is drawn across the middle,
In the far right-hand corner a pole is placed—

Ah, the telegraph wire across the field!

Now a wretched tumble-down house
Is built in the near left-hand corner,
With a narrow oblong window and dishevelled grass
below—

Your house, this?
Yes, and this is Daddy's window . . .

The white voids are impetuously scrawled with black
crayon—

It's night, it's night!
A cattle-thief! A burglar!
Dear me!
A goggle-eyed bogey,
Craning forward with arms dangling,
Comes reeling out from behind the telegraph pole—
Over the darkened field
And beneath the blossoms of stars.

Katsumi Tanaka

Chance Encounter

Halley's Comet appeared in 1910
(And I was born in the following year):
Its period being seventy-six years and seven days,
It is due to reappear in 1986—

So I read, and my heart sinks.
It is unlikely that I shall ever see the star—
And probably the case is the same with human encounters.

An understanding mind one meets as seldom,
And an undistracted love one wins as rarely—
I know that my true friend will appear after my death,
And my sweetheart died before I was born.

Wilderness

In the middle of a wilderness a band of wagons halted.
The season was mid-winter and the time was dusk.
Clouds in the sky were low: a sign of famine and plague.

In one of the wagons a man called Tsulu,
With brows deeply knit, was talking to himself:
'None of the princes would accept us;
And our Master [n] will give no thought
As to how my words fell flat, and why my ways were not
adopted.
Is it I am still deficient in Benevolence and Wisdom?
I am even chagrined at my Master's self-composure.'

In another wagon one called Tsukung,
Lifting his sagacious eyes, was talking to himself:
'None of the princes would accept us;
My reason tells me that my Master's way is great,
But my worldly wisdom says how easily
That greatness could be lopped, and therefore made
Acceptable to the general run of men . . .
I often resent my Master, and am then ashamed.'

In a third wagon was one called Yenyüan,[n]
Raising his greying head, he said:
'None of the princes would accept us;
And now I know this for a favourable sign.
For day by day I become more certain
That the True Way is unacceptable, and so are the truly
virtuous,
And I think myself most blessed, to die in the faith of
this Way and this Master.'

At that moment an old man in the middle wagon
Began to strum a lyre, reciting poems;
And the wilderness resounded with his voice and music.

Michizō Tachihara

Preface

Soft slow song,
From where do you come,
And where, after me,
Where will you fade?

In the evening glow
That closes the day,
When the sky starts to fill
With the murmur of stars,

Like a string whose tone
Is heightened to tears,
O tender song, what lodging in me?

And how send you back
To where you belong,
So late the hour, this lambent night?

NOTES

p. 15: *Like two bats in the birdless country*. In a birdless country the bat thinks himself important: cf. 'In the country of the blind the one-eyed man is king'.

p. 22: *Yamato*. The present-day Kansai: the description is of Hōryūji near Nara.

p. 25: *Home Thoughts*. The poem is about Kyoto. The Mibu farce (*Mibu-kyōgen*) is a religious pantomime dating back to 1299 which is performed during ten days in April at Mibudera Temple.

p. 29: *diamant glass jar*. Possibly electric light bulb; the following lines may refer to the magic lantern.
putrid petrolic oil. Oil paint must have seemed a nasty if fascinating concoction as compared with the native ink-stick and water.

p. 30: *Okaru and Kampei*. A famous pair of lovers, from the story of the Forty-seven *Rōnin* (*Chūshingura*), popular as a *Kabuki* play and (as here) a puppet play.

p. 31: *samisen*. Three-stringed instrument with small square sound-box and long neck.

p. 32: *abóbora*. Portuguese for pumpkin. Kitahara, like other Japanese writers, makes great play with foreign words, partly for the exotic effect.

p. 37: *Roshō*. A singer of *gidayū*, the ballads chanted in puppet plays.

p. 38: *Yotsume*. Famous for its Peony Garden.

p. 39: *Gandhara*. Ancient Gandhara in north-western India, with its Greco-Buddhist art.
'Yellow Earth' civilization. Northern Chinese, Han Dynasty.

p. 49: *hōku*. Japanese version of the word 'fork'. We have left it untranslated because the rather self-conscious use of the foreign eating implement (with something of the same associations that chopsticks have for us) is part of the 'special occasion' here enjoyed. Cf. drinking *sake* from a western tumbler in Kinoshita's poem on p. 38.

p. 52: *Susaki Waterfront*. Southern part of Tokyo, along the Bay, it was known for its brothels.

p. 54: *Samma*. Mackerel-pike. Broiled on a gridiron, this is a popular plain dish, especially in Tokyo; the guts are considered a delicacy on account of their bitterness. The word has been left untranslated because of its altogether different associations. The Japanese are great connoisseurs of fish, which they take so seriously that *samma*, for example, can be invoked without incongruity in a highly personal poem.

p. 57: *De-kli-na-tion*. Declension. A German lesson is in progress nearby.

p. 59: *world of the Asura*. One of the six worlds of transmigration, this is filled with hatred and jealousy, for the souls there must fight one another without cease as a punishment for the violence committed in their previous life, until they have worked out their karma.

p. 64: *haori*. A short coat worn over kimono.
rubashka. Russian-style jacket.
the Ginza. The thoroughfare which is the shopping and entertainment centre of Tokyo.

p. 66: *and other such names*. That is, the names of modern poets.

p. 67: *with the figure of a gazelle*. The animal invoked in the original poem is the giraffe: another case of dissimilar associations.

p. 77: *In our language you contain a 'mother' in you*. The written character for 'sea' contains the character for 'mother'.

p. 80: *kappa*. 'River-child', a water-sprite very prominent in Japanese folk-lore. He has a hollow on the top of the skull, filled with water, which gives him great strength. When wrestling with a *kappa*, you must contrive to spill this water, otherwise he will drag you down into the river.

p. 87: *shōji*. Sliding door or wall made of paper framed in wood.

p. 91: *our Master* . i.e Confucius.

p. 92: *Yenyüan*. Better known as Yen Hui, Confucius' favourite disciple. The incident related in this poem is given by Ssu-ma Ch'ien in his *Shih Chi*.

BIOGRAPHICAL NOTES

TŌSON SHIMAZAKI (1872–1943)

Youngest son of a scholar of Japanese classical literature. He was educated at a mission college in Tokyo and baptized. Later taught at a mission college in Sendai. Also distinguished as a novelist. He represented Japan at the International P.E.N. Conference in Buenos Aires in 1936.

BANSUI TSUCHII (1871–1952)

Mostly self-educated, though he later graduated from the English Department of Tokyo (Imperial) University. Spent three years in England, France, Germany and Italy. Late in life he was made a Freeman of Sendai City, whereupon he adopted the more popular reading of his family name, Doi. Essayist and translator, notably of the *Iliad* and *Odyssey*.

KYŪKIN SUSUKIDA (1877–1945)

His education was chiefly acquired in Ueno Library, the largest Tokyo library of Japanese classical literature. Later worked for the Osaka *Mainichi* newspaper. He published five volumes of poetry, the last in his thirtieth year.

ARIAKE KAMBARA (1876–1952)

Published four books of poems, the last at the age of thirty-two, and thereafter occupied himself in revising them. His first name is sometimes read as Yūmei.

HAKUSHŪ KITAHARA (1885–1942)

Born in Kyūshū, in which dialect he later wrote many poems. Besides his work in the modern style he wrote *tanka*, folk-poems and nursery rhymes.

ROFŪ MIKI (b. 1889)

Studied at both Waseda and Keiō universities (Tokyo). Edited several magazines successively. Later entered a Trappist monastery in Hokkaidō temporarily.

MOKUTARŌ KINOSHITA (1885–1945)

His real name was Masao Ōta. A graduate of the Medical Department of Tokyo University, he took his M.D. with a study of leprosy (for which he was later awarded the *Légion d'honneur*). Besides two *Kabuki* plays, he published two books of poetry.

KŌTARŌ TAKAMURA (1883–1956)

Eldest son of the famous sculptor, Kōun Takamura. After graduating from Tokyo Art Academy, he spent three years abroad, in America, England and France.

BOCHŌ YAMAMURA (1884–1924)

Started as an uncertificated school-teacher. He studied English under a missionary and then graduated from the Holy Trinity Theological College in Tokyo. Working as a priest, he suffered from tuberculosis and poverty. A quasi-surrealist to begin with, he finally turned into a 'nature poet'.

SAKUTARŌ HAGIWARA (1886–1942)

An important theorist (*The Poetic Principle*, 1928) as well as practitioner. Of his essays in Nietzschean aphorism, *Fictitious Justice* (1929) was particularly popular.

SAISEI MURŌ (b. 1889)

Completely self-educated after junior high school. Together with his friend Hagiwara, he published a poetry magazine *Feeling*. He has also written several realistic novels.

HARUO SATŌ (b. 1892)

Left the Department of Literature of Keiō University without finishing the course. He began his career as a novelist, and has published nearly seventy books of criticism, translations (including Chinese women poets) and fiction. The definitive *Collected Poems* came out in 1952.

KENJI MIYAZAWA (1896–1933)

Born in Northern Japan, he was a devout Buddhist, an agriculturalist and a chemist. The greater part of his numerous poems and fairy tales was published posthumously.

SHINKICHI TAKAHASHI (b. 1901)

After leaving secondary school he worked as a journalist on a local newspaper. In 1921 he passed six months in a Buddhist monastery. He then declared himself a Dadaist and began to write poems. His *Collected Poems* came out in 1952.

SHIGEHARU NAKANO (b. 1902)

While studying German literature at Tokyo University he joined the 'New People's Association', a Marxist organization, and in 1928 he helped to found the 'Japan Federation of Proletarian Artists'. He was imprisoned several times. Since 1930 he has been more active as a novelist, critic and politician (from 1947 to 1950 he sat in the House of Councillors as a Communist member), but he remains the best of the 'socialist' poets. *Collected Poems* was published in 1931.

TŌSABURŌ ONO (b. 1903)

A native of Osaka, he attended the Tōyō University in Tokyo for a while. While young he set up as an anarchist but chiefly concerned himself with literary theory. No longer an anarchist, he remains a firm opponent of traditional poetic forms and subjects.

FUYUE ANZAI (b. 1898)

Lived in Dairen, Manchuria, from 1919 till 1934; founded, with Fuyuhiko Kitagawa, the poetry magazine *A* (for Asia). Has published six books of poems and one of essays. He now works in Osaka Municipal Office and also teaches.

FUYUHIKO KITAGAWA (b. 1900)

Went to Manchuria as a boy of ten. He has been actively associated with a number of magazines. He once wrote, 'I started with Dadaistic poems, followed with Surrealistic, and have finally reached Neo-realism. I may seem changeable, but I am sure I have been consistent in my will to get, through poetry, at the innermost human spirit in its social aspect.'

IKU TAKENAKA (b. 1904)

A native of Kobe, he graduated from the English Department of Kansei Gakuin University. In 1924 he started a magazine called *The Compass* for the Sea-port Poets' Club. Has travelled a good deal in Europe, and knew Cocteau, Man Ray, etc., in France.

JUN YAMAMURA (b. 1898)

Born in Tokyo and educated at a commercial school in Osaka. He collaborated with Iku Takenaka in *The Compass*. Has published five books of poetry.

TATSUJI MIYOSHI (b. 1900)

Born in Osaka. His early ambition was to be a soldier and he entered the Military Academy; later he changed his mind and enrolled in the French Department of Tokyo University. He started his poetic career under the influence of Sakutarō Hagiwara and Saisei Murō: 'it was these two poets . . . who rejected the marshalling of flowery words . . . and spoke about daily matters from the very bottom of their unaffected, urgent, feeling hearts'. One of the founders of the magazine *Four Seasons*, which represents the main current in the lyrical tradition of modern Japanese poetry.

JUNZABURŌ NISHIWAKI (b. 1894)

After graduating in economics at Keiō University, he studied English literature at Oxford; his first book of poems was published in London, *Spectrum* (1925). He has written a number of books on European literature and translated Eliot's *The Waste Land* into Japanese. At present he is Professor of English literature at Keiō University.

SHIMPEI KUSANO (b. 1903)

He went to China at the age of eighteen and graduated from Lingnan University in Canton, returning to Japan in 1939. *The Hundredth Class* (1928) attracted attention: it was all about frogs, whom the poet held to be 'great admirers of Nature', 'the ditch-smelling proletariat', 'cheerful anarchists' and 'the living heaven'.

SHŪZŌ HISHIYAMA (b. 1909)

A native of Tokyo, he studied at the University of Foreign Studies there. He is supposed to represent the Intellectual school; has translated French authors, including Valéry (in chronological order).

SUMAKO FUKAO (b. 1893)

The only woman poet in this anthology; and the only one (outside the traditionalists) to establish herself as a major figure. At nineteen she married an undergraduate poet with whom she studied 'Japanese classics, Baudelaire and Browning, Nietzsche and Schopenhauer, and Russian literature . . .' On her husband's death eight years later she compiled a volume of his poems, which she followed in quick succession with several of her own. *Collected Poems* came out in 1952.

KAORU MARUYAMA (b. 1899)

He studied for some time at the Higher Mercantile Marine School, then changed to the Japanese Literature Department of Tokyo University. Was one of the editors of *Four Seasons*. He lives in Toyohashi and lectures at Aichi University.

FUYUJI TANAKA (b. 1894)

Born in Northern Japan, he worked in a bank for thirty-six years until his retirement in 1949. Has published about eleven books of verse.

SHIZUO ITŌ (1906–1953)

Born in Kyūshū, he studied Japanese literature at Kyoto (Imperial) University. Published four collections of poetry.

KATSUMI TANAKA (b. 1911)

He read Oriental history at Tokyo University. His first book was a translation of Novalis, *Blue Flowers*. He is now a teacher and lives in Osaka.

MICHIZŌ TACHIHARA (1914–1949)

An architect by profession, he began his poetic career as a disciple of Saisei Murō and was connected with the *Four Seasons* group.